STARS OF SPORTS

CHAD KERLEY

BMX'S BREAKOUT STAR

by Matt Chandler

CAPSTONE EDITIONS
a capstone imprint

Stars of Sports is published by Capstone Press, an imprint of Capstone
1710 Roe Crest Drive, North Mankato, Minnesota 56003
www.capstonepub.com

**Library of Congress Cataloging-in-Publication Data is available
on the Library of Congress website.**

ISBN: 978-1-4966-9527-7 (library binding)
ISBN: 978-1-9771-5397-5 (eBook PDF)

Summary: At just four years old, Chad Kerley knew he was destined to spend life on
a bike. But despite a successful career as a competitive BMX racer, by age 13, CK was
ready to give it all up. Kerley quit racing and went back to riding for fun. He eventually
returned to the world of BMX with a new style—freestyle—and proved he was stronger
than ever.

Image Credits
Getty Images: Allen Berezovsky, 9, Allen J. Schaben, 8, Harry How, 27, HECTOR
RETAMAL, 28, Icon Sports Wire, 7, Robert Benson, 13, Thananuwat Srirasant, 17,
25; Newscom: Alejandro Garcia/EFE, 16, Anthony Souffle/ZUMA Press, Cover, 5, 21,
23, Ashley Landis/ZUMA Press, 19, Earnie Grafton/ZUMA Press, 12, LEJANDRO
GARCIA/EFE, 11, Mark Holtzman/ZUMA Press, 14, 15; Shutterstock: Dancestrokes, 6,
Vladimir Arndt, 1

Editorial Credits
Editor: Alison Deering; Designer: Elyse White; Media Researcher: Morgan Walters;
Production Specialist: Spencer Rosio

All internet sites appearing in back matter were available and accurate when this book
was sent to press.

Direct Quotations
Page 7, from May 9, 2012, AlliSports video "Chad Kerley BMX Alli Show,"
https://www.youtube.com
Page 7, from May 10, 2012, *Complex* article, "Ambitions as a Rider: How Chad Kerley Is
Changing BMX," https://www.complex.com
Page 8, from May 9, 2012, AlliSports video "Chad Kerley BMX Alli Show,"
https://www.youtube.com
Page 11, from Premium BMX team page, https://premiumbmx.com
Page 15, from June 30, 2012, *Los Angeles Daily News* article, "X Games Notebook:
Reynolds wins 5th straight BMX Street title; Sablone has planned victory; Rallycross
driver hospitalized," https://www.dailynews.com
Page 26, from June 6, 2014, BET article, "BMX Rider Chad Kerley Gears Up for X
Games Austin," https://www.bet.com

TABLE OF CONTENTS

Glossary terms are **BOLD** on first use.

STREET GOLD

Chad Kerley sat on his bike at the top of the ramp. It was the X Games 2018 in Minneapolis, Minnesota. Kerley was in second place. He trailed fellow American Garrett Reynolds by two points. He needed at least 91.34 points (out of 100) for a chance at the gold medal.

Kerley took off on his bike. He landed a **barspin** to **ice pick grind** combo early. He followed that with a pair of **feebles**. The crowd cheered as he landed a pair of **nose wheelies** and a **360**.

Kerley saved his best for last. He jumped his bike and landed a nose wheelie on the rail. His run earned him a score of 92.33. He had won the gold medal!

>>> Kerley competes in the BMX Street Final at the X Games in Minneapolis, Minnesota, in 2018.

CHAPTER ONE

YOUNG RACER

Chad Kerley—CK, as he's known to most—was born in San Diego, California, on January 27, 1994. He got his first BMX bike when he was just four years old.

Kerley was a natural. His dad, Randy, began to enter him in competitive BMX races close to home.

>>> Downtown San Diego, California

〉〉〉 Bikers compete in the 2007 UCI BMX World Championship.

As a young racer, Kerley dominated. By the time he was 13, he'd won first place in his district five times. He was a two-time state champion in California. He placed second in the 2006 UCI BMX World Championship.

Kerley was on his way to a career as a professional BMX racer. Then, at age 13, he quit.

RIDING AWAY

The decision to quit racing was tough. Kerley's dad wasn't happy. He wanted his son to keep racing and turn pro.

Kerley still loved to be on his bike. But he had grown tired of competitive racing. He wanted the chance to ride for fun and be a kid.

> "I started riding in a skate park," he said. "It was more of a stress-free environment when I started freestyle. I wasn't going up against anybody, I was just having fun on my bike."

〉〉〉 Kerley soars over a jump, hands-free, during the X Games in Los Angeles, California, in 2013.

>>> Kerley attends a premiere in Venice, California, in 2008.

BMX freestyle is a different world than racing. In racing, every competitor follows the same track. Freestyle racers are given a set time and are free to do whatever tricks they want. Kerley was looking for more fun, and he found it in BMX freestyle.

CHAPTER TWO

STREET RIDER

An important part of freestyle is the making of street videos. Street riders perform tricks in public spaces. These tricks can be done on man-made obstacles such as curbs, handrails, stairs, and ledges.

Kerley and his friends made videos of his rides and tricks and shared them online. Those videos helped him gain fans and sponsors, including companies like Premium BMX.

Backyard Boss

When Kerley was 15 years old, Premium BMX helped pay to have a custom ramp built in his backyard! The ramp was roughly 50 feet (15 meters) long. It allowed Kerley to perfect his tricks without leaving home. His backyard soon became a hangout for professional riders from across the community.

Kerley quickly became an **elite** BMX freestyle rider. He spent two years as an **amateur**. Then, in 2010, he turned pro. Sponsors paid Kerley to ride. He also competed against other pro riders in competitions.

〉〉〉 Kerley competes in Barcelona, Spain, in 2013.

RETURN TO COMPETITION

By 2011, Kerley was once again making a name for himself. At just 17 years old, he joined the Dew Tour, an extreme sports competition. At one stop in Portland, Oregon, Kerley landed a **manual** into a **hang five**. The combo is considered very difficult to land back to back. Kerley made it look easy.

The teen sensation didn't slow down as the year went on. In between competitions, Kerley continued to make videos for his sponsors. He traveled the country creating new, more daring tricks.

〉〉〉 Skateboarder Tony Hawk wows the crowd at a skatepark in Clairemont, near San Diego, California.

The highlight of the year came at Simple Session 2011 in Estonia. Kerley finished eighth in the overall competition but won Best Trick with a two-rail routine. He pulled an up-ledge ride to ice pick on the rail. He perfectly carried it into a manual, to barspin, to ice pick down the ledge.

Skate Style

There are many similarities between freestyle BMX and skateboarding. The ramps are similar, both skateboarding and BMX use similar tricks, and athletes build a following using social media videos. There are a lot of crossover athletes between the sports. When he was a young racer, Kerley traveled to skateparks, including the Clairemont Skatepark, to ride. He developed his best tricks as he rode alongside skaters.

2012 X GAMES

Kerley competed in his first U.S. X Games in Los Angeles, California, in 2012, just one week after graduating from high school. He was 18 years old and an underdog.

In the end, it was Kerley and Garrett Reynolds fighting for the gold. Reynolds had won gold in every X Games street event since it began. Kerley held a one-point lead after their first runs. But Reynolds delivered a strong second run to take the lead.

〉〉〉 The skatepark at the 2012 X Games in Los Angeles, California

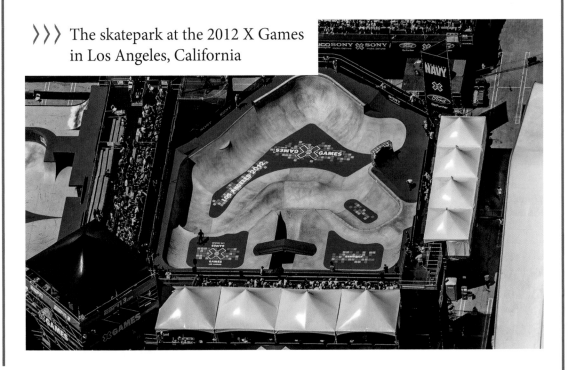

〉〉〉 A ramp at X Games 18, as seen from above

In his final run, Kerley landed everything from a **540** to a nose wheelie along the rail. He climbed the wall and dazzled the crowd with his style. It wasn't quite enough. Reynolds won the gold, even though he thought Kerley deserved it.

"If I were a judge, I would've given it to him," Reynolds said after the finals. *"The dude is crazy."*

Kerley hoped to build on the **momentum** from his silver medal. He finished his 2012 season strong. He placed second at the Dew Tour event in San Francisco, California. He won the Texas Toast Jam.

That same year, Kerley was named Freestyler of the Year by *BMX Plus Magazine*. His incredible year also included the Vital BMX Rider of the Year award and the Nora Cup People's Choice Rider of the Year award.

Despite all that, Kerley was an underdog going into the 2013 X Games. No rider had been able to take the gold medal from five-time winner Reynolds. Kerley knew he would have to do something special if he wanted to be the first.

>>> Kerley shows off his BMX skills at the X Games in Barcelona, Spain.

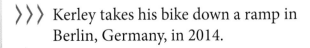

>>> Kerley takes his bike down a ramp in Berlin, Germany, in 2014.

CHAPTER FOUR
KING OF THE STREET

With a gold medal under his belt, Kerley was at the top of the BMX street riding game. He had done what no one else could. He had taken the gold from Reynolds. Expectations were high. Could Kerley live up to the hype?

Fresh from his gold-medal win, Kerley headed east to compete in the Mongoose Jam. He carried the momentum from the 2013 X Games into the competition and delivered another big win!

Kerley's success declined in the following years, though. He finished a disappointing eighth place at X Games Austin 2014. He added a seventh-place finish at X Games Austin 2016, followed by an eighth-place finish at X Games Minneapolis 2017.

But Kerley never gave up. He trained hard. He kept competing. And in 2018, he made a comeback.

>>> Kerley competes in the BMX Street Final at the 2018 X Games in Minneapolis, Minnesota.

BACK ON THE PODIUM

Kerley returned to form at X Games Minneapolis 2018. He beat out 11 other riders in the finals to win gold. His final score of 92.33 points was enough to beat 12-time gold-medal winner Garrett Reynolds, who took the silver.

Kerley didn't stop there. In 2019, he traveled to Shanghai, China, for another round of X Games. Kerley was determined to win a medal. He closed out his final ride with a **switch tail** and went straight into a 540. He executed both perfectly. His final run earned him the bronze.

Later that year, Kerley returned to Minneapolis for X Games 2019. He brought home another bronze medal for BMX street.

It was the sixth X Games medal of Kerley's young career. He is one of just three people to win BMX street gold since the event was added in 2008.

>>> Kerley performs a trick for the crowd at the 2018 X Games, where he took home the gold.

CHAPTER FIVE

OFF THE BIKE

Kerley loves to ride. He even organized his own BMX event. He held the Chad Kerley Invitational in Chicago, Illinois, in 2012. Amateur riders competed for $20,000 in prize money!

But Kerley is more than just a BMX street rider. He also loves music. Rapping is one of his favorite hobbies. Like everything he does, Kerley takes his music seriously. When he isn't riding, he sometimes stays up all night writing and recording. He even performed live at the House of Blues in San Diego.

Kerley also collects sneakers. He was even sponsored by Nike at one time. According to Kerley, he has 300 to 500 pairs.

FACT

Kerley helped design his own custom line of bike parts called Premium CK.

〉〉〉 In 2018, Kerley came in second in BMX Street Rink, which was held in Berlin, Germany.

THE FUTURE FOR CK

While there are professional BMX riders as old as 40, it is still a young person's sport. Kerley is in his prime. But injuries and age can wear a rider down. Kerley has dealt with back issues because of his riding. He once suffered a broken jaw and lost six teeth in a crash.

Kerley plays down his injuries. "I've had some minor breaks here and there, but it's all part of the sport," he said.

As for a time when he can no longer ride his bike, Kerley has options. He has already made appearances in multiple Hollywood films. He can continue to develop bikes and accessories for the next generation of riders. He has even talked about pursuing music when his riding days are done.

⟩⟩⟩ Kerley performs a hands-free trick at X Games Los Angeles in 2013.

GLOSSARY

360 (three-SIX-tee)—a complete spin

540 (fahyv-FAWR-tee)—a spin with one and a half rotations

AMATEUR (AM-uh-chur)—an athlete not paid for playing a sport

BARSPIN (bahr-spin)—when a rider spins the bike's handlebars around while in the air and catches them before landing

ELITE (i-LEET)—the best in the league

FEEBLE (FEE-buhl)—a basic grind that involves a bike's front wheel riding along a ledge while the rear peg grinds on it

HANG FIVE (hang fahyv)—a front-wheel balance done with a rider's front foot on the peg and back leg swinging back and forth for balance

HEAT (HEET)—a single race in a contest that includes two or more races

ICE PICK GRIND (ahys PIK GRINDE)—a grind done on a bike's rear peg

MANUAL (MAN-yoo-uhl)—a BMX trick done by riding on just the back wheel while not turning the pedals

MOMENTUM (moh-MEN-tuhm)—the speed created by movement

NOSE WHEELIE (NOHZ WEE-lee)—a stand performed on a bike's front wheel

SWITCH TAIL (SWICH TAYL)—when a rider jumps off the bike in the air, then kicks the bike into a full spin, landing back on it

READ MORE

Butterfield, Moira, and Kath Jewitt. *Kids' Cycling Handbook: Tips, Facts and Know-How About Road, Track, BMX and Mountain Biking*. New York: Carlton Books, 2016.

Hale, K.A. *BMX Racing*. Minnetonka, MN: Kaleidoscope Publishing, Inc., 2020.

Whiting, Jim. *BMX*. Mankato, MN: Creative Education, 2018.

INTERNET SITES

Best of BMX at the X Games
xgames.com/video/bmx

BMX on the Dew Tour
dewtour.com/tag/bmx/

Kerley's Bio for Haro Bikes
harobikes.com/pages/chad-kerley

INDEX